DAN COATES Plays Easy Piano Selections From

THE SECRET GARDEN

CONTENTS

(800) 876-9777   (800) 892-9777
10075 SW Beav-Hills Hwy (503) 641-5691
733 SW 10th (503) 228-6659
19151 NE Burnside (503) 667-4663

Cover Art by Doug Johnson © 1991

DAN COATES

DAN COATES is perhaps the most widely acclaimed name in the field of printed music. Equally adept in arranging for beginners or accomplished musicians, his publications have been enthusiastically received by teachers and professionals nationwide.

Born in Syracuse, New York, Dan began to play piano at age four. By the time he was fifteen, he'd won a New York State competition for music composers. After high school graduation, he toured the United States, Canada and Europe as arranger and pianist with the world famous group "Up With People".

Dan settled in Miami, Florida, where he studied piano with Ivan Davis at the University of Miami, while playing professionally throughout the South Florida area. Dan's unique piano arrangements became the talk of the entertainment field, and as he began to publish, his fame grew. In 1982, Dan began his association with Warner Bros. Music.

A very busy and talented songwriter/arranger, Dan currently lives and works in the Los Angeles area. Throughout the year, he conducts piano workshops around the country, where piano teachers and students attend to hear him demonstrate his popular arrangements.

THE GIRL I MEAN TO BE

Lyrics by
MARSHA NORMAN

Music by
LUCY SIMON
Arranged by DAN COATES

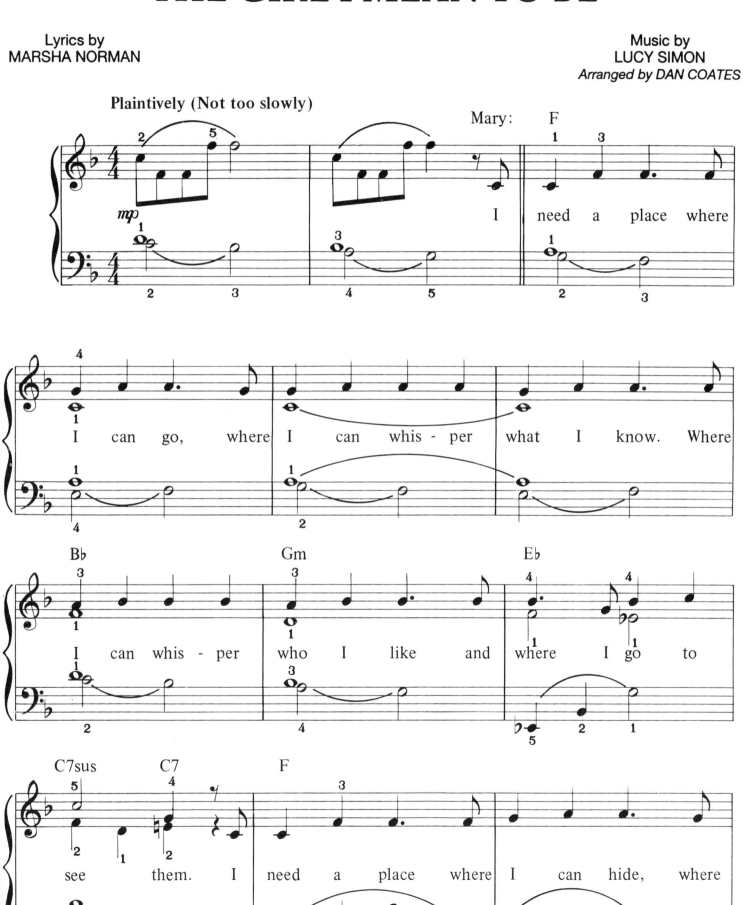

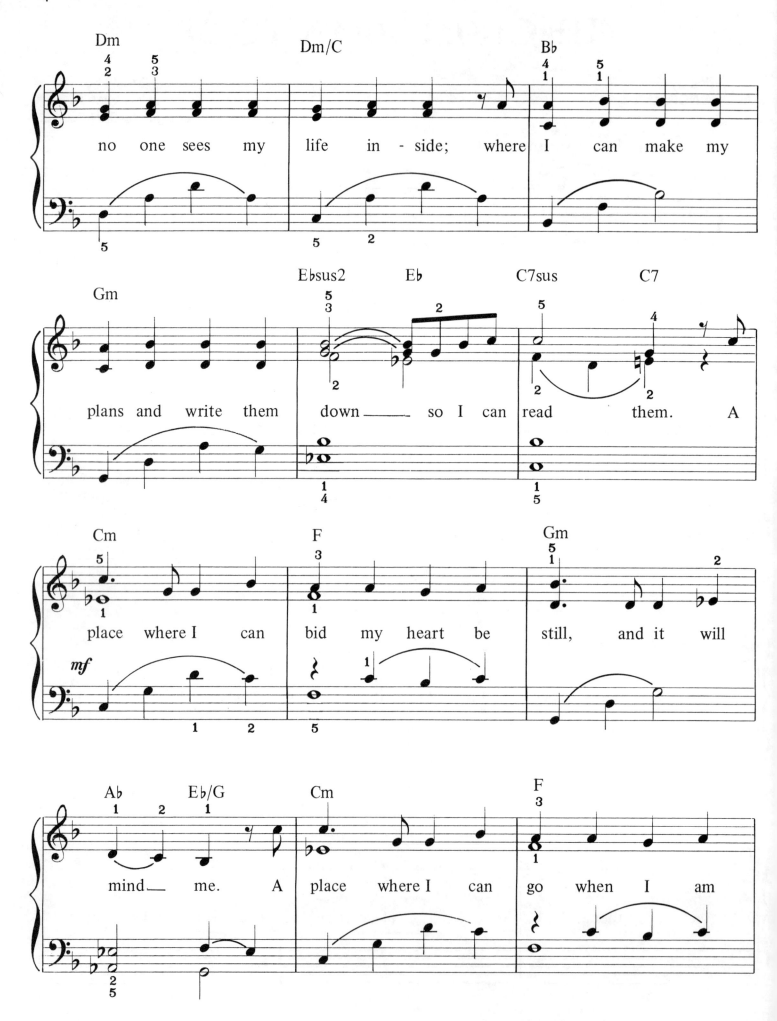

lost and there I'll find me. I
need a place to spend the day, where no one says to
go or stay. Where I can take my pen and draw the girl I
mean to be.

COME TO MY GARDEN

Lyrics by
MARSHA NORMAN

Moderately slow

Music by
LUCY SIMON
Arranged by DAN COATES

A BIT OF EARTH

Lyrics by
MARSHA NORMAN

Music by
LUCY SIMON
Arranged by DAN COATES

2.

Cm7/F   F7   B♭

earth   to make   it   live.____

(more forcefully)   G/A   Gm/A
D/A

She   should   have   a   po — ny   gal - lop 'cross   the

f

with pedal

Em7/A   A7   D/A   G/A

moor.   She   should   have   a   doll's   house   with a

Gm/A   D/A   Bm   F♯m/A

hun - dred rooms per   floor.   Why   can't she ask   for a   *mf*

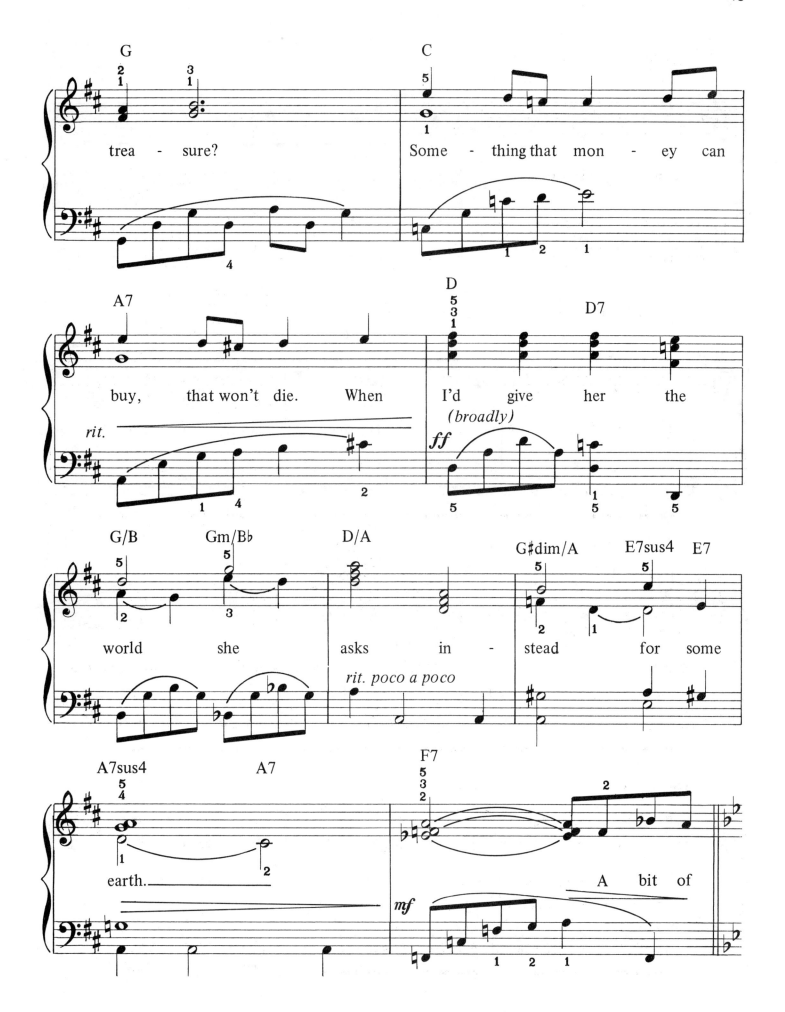

a tempo

earth... She wants a lit - tle bit of earth, she'll plant some

seeds.____ The seeds will grow, the flow - ers

bloom, their beau - ty just the thing she needs.____

She'll grow to love____ the ten-der ros - es, lil - ies fair, the i - ris

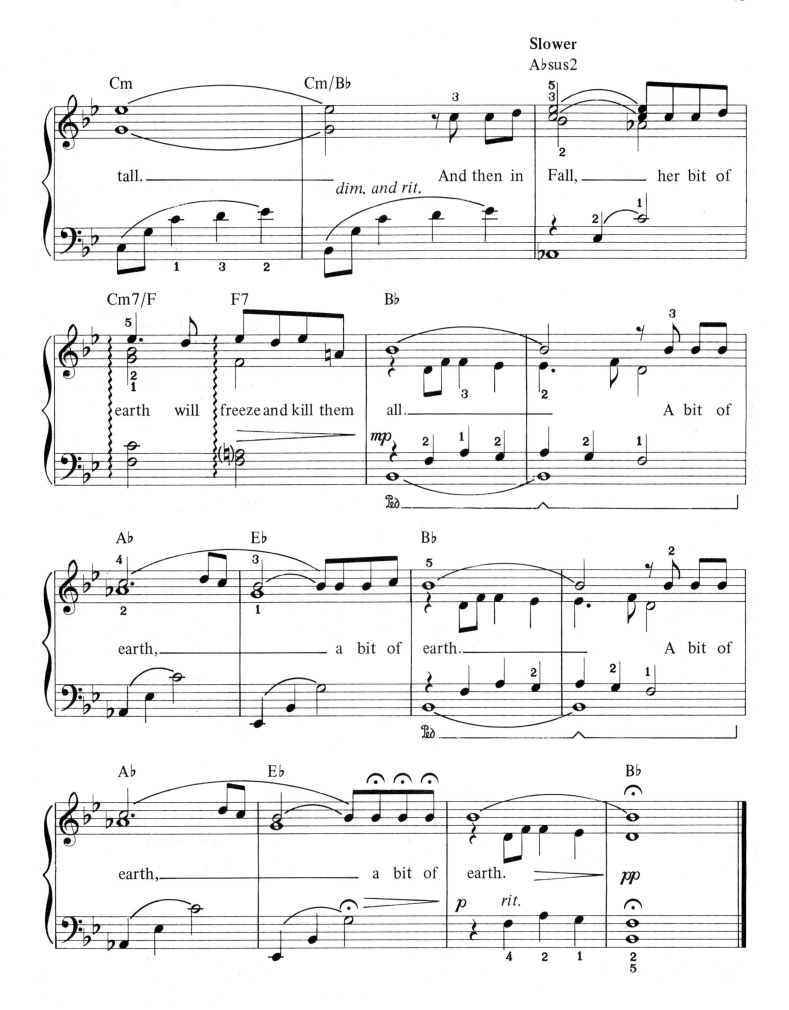

HOLD ON

Lyrics by
MARSHA NORMAN

Music by
LUCY SIMON
Arranged by DAN COATES

LILY'S EYES

Lyrics by
MARSHA NORMAN

Music by
LUCY SIMON
Arranged by DAN COATES

Moderately, with movement

Dr. Craven:

She has her

F(addG)   F   Bb

eyes.   The girl has Li - ly's ha - zel eyes.   Those

Gm7(b5)   C7sus   C7

eyes that saw him hap - py long a - go.   Those

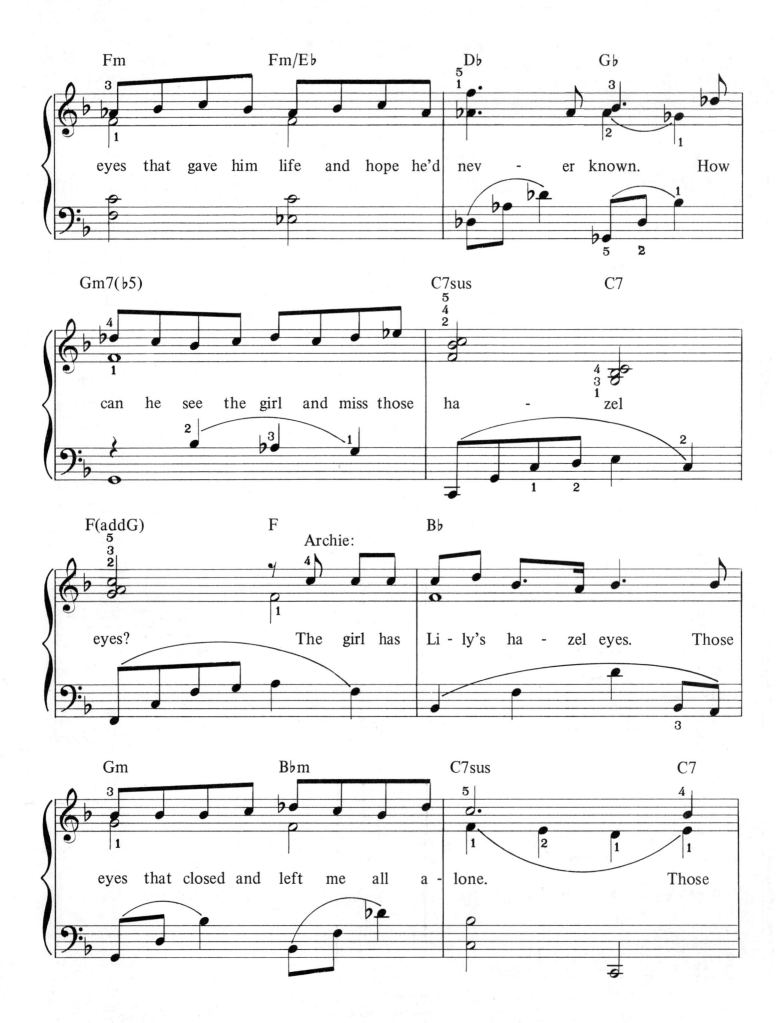

RACE YOU TO THE TOP
OF THE MORNING

Lyrics by
MARSHA NORMAN

Music by
LUCY SIMON
Arranged by DAN COATES

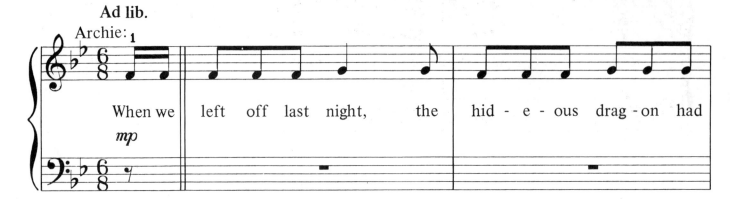

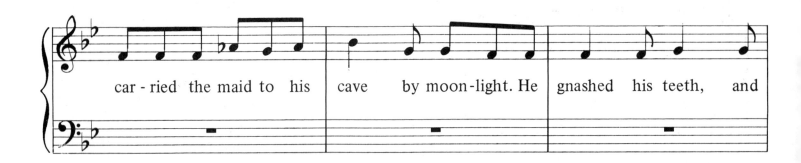

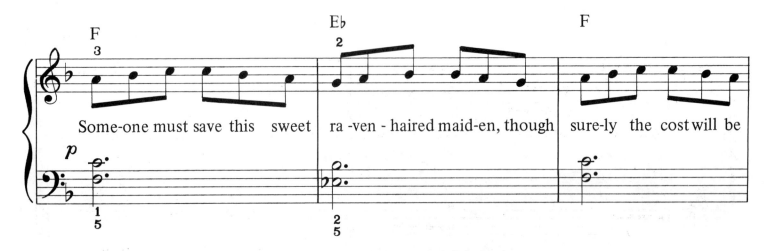

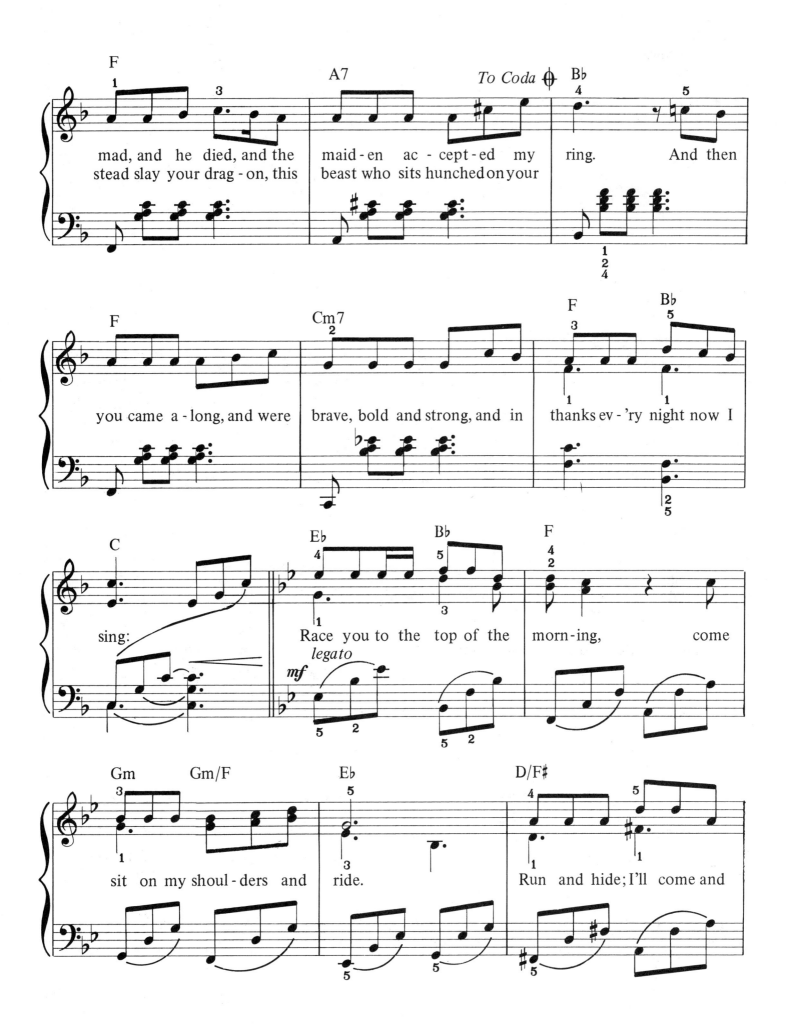

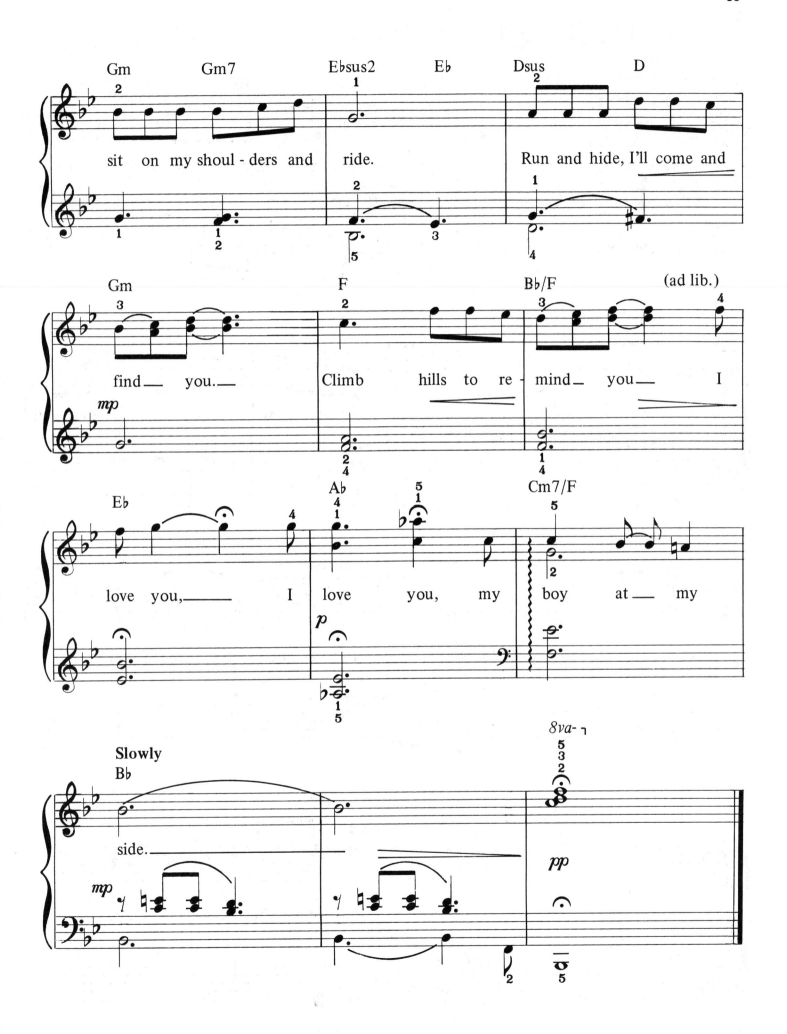

HOW COULD I EVER KNOW?

Lyrics by
MARSHA NORMAN

Music by
LUCY SIMON
Arranged by DAN COATES

IF I HAD A FINE WHITE HORSE

Lyrics by
MARSHA NORMAN

Music by
LUCY SIMON
Arranged by DAN COATES

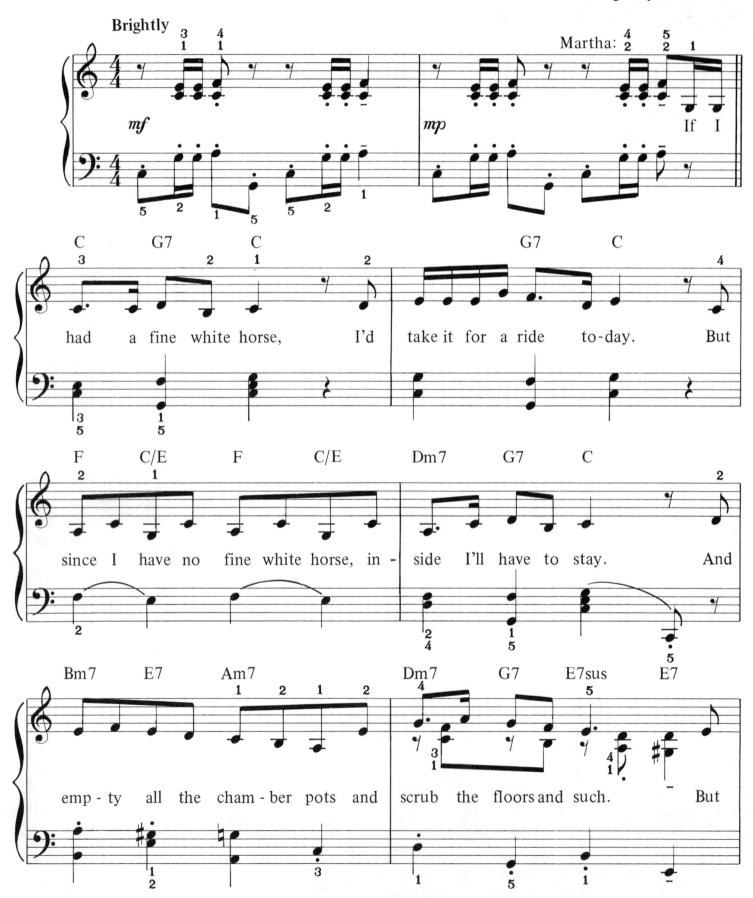

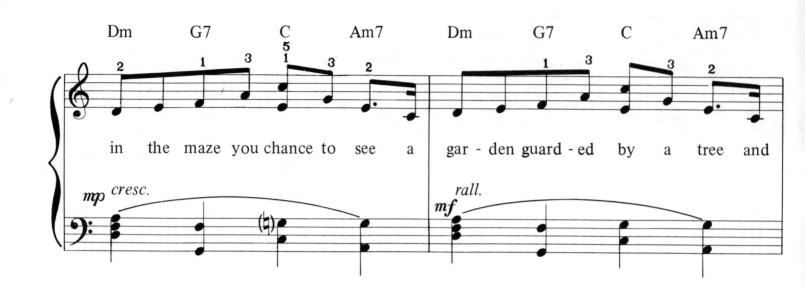

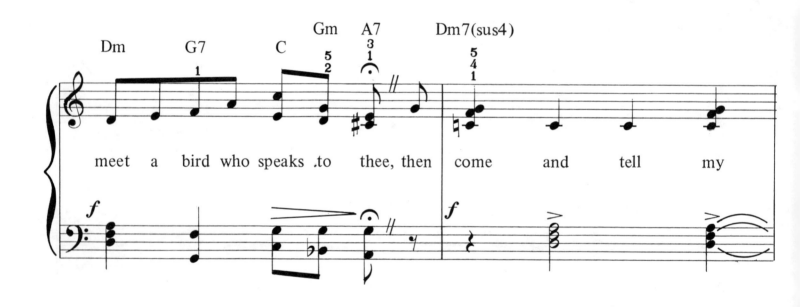